JOHNNY CASH

WALKING ON FIRE

Publisher and Creative Director: Nick Wells

Project Editor: Polly Prior

Picture Research: Matt Knight and Polly Prior

Art Director and Layout Design: Jane Ashley

Digital Design and Production: Chris Herbert

Copy Editor: Claire Baranowski

Proofreader: Dawn Laker

Special thanks to: Laura Bulbeck, Stephen Feather, Michael Heatley

FLAME TREE PUBLISHING

Crabtree Hall, Crabtree Lane

Fulham, London SW6 6TY

United Kingdom

www.flametreepublishing.com

www.flametreerock.com

First published 2015

10 12 14 13 11

1 3 5 7 9 10 8 6 4 2

A CIP record for this book is available from the British Library upon request.

ISBN 978-1-78361-313-7

Printed in China

JOHNNY CASH

WALKING ON FIRE

HELEN AKITT

Foreword: Paul Du Noyer

**FLAME TREE
PUBLISHING**

CONTENTS

FOREWORD

First there was the voice. Johnny Cash sang in a sour growl that was full of hurt but free of self-pity. It rumbled up from subterranean depths like a lazy volcano, but was still supremely human. The effect was of a perpetual war between hope and self-destruction. He could overawe the toughest convict crowd because they could hear in his voice their own daily struggle for dignity. Johnny Cash sang like a man battling passions he could not trust himself to master.

Then there was the rhythm – that famous 'boom-chicka-boom' – trotting up to you like a faithful hound. Cash was a country singer to his bones, yet his music seethed with a kind of internalized wildness, and rock'n'rollers have always recognized him for a kindred spirit. Elvis Presley was his friend, Bob Dylan embraced him like a brother, acts like U2 and Nick Cave queued to work with him. In his last years, he had an all-purpose cool that saw him lionized by fans from Nashville to Glastonbury.

Finally, there were the songs. They might be funny or sad, angry or romantic. But Cash's world-view was rooted in real life and hard-won experience. He'd been a lover and a drunk, a junkie and a patriot, a car-wrecker and a God-fearing son of the poverty-stricken South. Whether he sang of guns, heartbreak, the jailhouse or Jesus, Johnny Cash was not just versatile, he was all-encompassing. Both rootsy and adventurous, with a grave authority that defied disbelief, the 'Man in Black' was a whole continent in one body.

Paul Du Noyer

Editor, writer and rock musicologist

HELLO, I'M JOHNNY CASH

'I DIDN'T JUST SING ABOUT COTTON; I KNEW COTTON.'
JOHNNY CASH

At once both understated and complex, Johnny Cash survived a roller-coaster 50-year career and transcended his 1950s country-and-western roots to become a popular music icon continually appealing to new generations. He is remembered as a groundbreaking figure in a number of musical genres, from country through to gospel to rock'n'roll.

'Hello, I'm Johnny Cash,' was his trademark self-deprecating introduction when he took to yet another stage in his long and eventful career. The self-styled 'Man in Black' became one of the most influential musicians of the twentieth century, writing over 1,000 songs, recording twice that number, and releasing over 90 million discs.

From his early life in the cotton fields of Arkansas, Cash would travel to Sun studios in Memphis, following in the footsteps of Elvis, and on to the centre of country music itself, Nashville, Tennessee. He would release nearly 100 studio albums and sell records worldwide.

Cry, Cry, Cry

Cash's early single on Sun Records, 'Cry, Cry, Cry', cracked the country chart, but it was the 1956 chart-topping single 'I Walk The Line' that crossed over to the pop Top 20 and made the world stand up and listen. This rockabilly-style country song sold over two million copies and put the Man in Black on the musical map. Much later, it was the title of an Oscar-winning Hollywood biopic starring Joaquin Phoenix in the title role.

His marriage to his first wife, Vivian, fell victim to his rock'n'roll lifestyle of touring and drug-taking (Cash loved touring, and in later years used a special tour bus he called 'Unit One' when touring in North America). His second wife, June Carter, who he married in 1968, proved to be a stabilizing influence on his addictive personality and saved him from self-destruction on many occasions. They toured and recorded together, and would die within months of each other in 2003. Although Cash fought his demons daily for much of his life, he produced music right up until his death.

'BEFORE ROCK'N'ROLL THERE WAS COUNTRY AND BEFORE MEMPHIS [FOR ME] THERE WAS ARKANSAS.'

JOHNNY CASH

The Man Comes Around

In his later years, Cash worked with cutting-edge talents such as producer Rick Rubin, songwriter Trent Reznor of Nine Inch Nails and video director Anton Corbijn, a close collaborator with U2. Dragging himself up from a personal and musical decline in the 1980s, he successfully reinvented himself to capture a new audience.

The Man Comes Around, released in 2002, was Cash's final complete studio album, and proved to be a fitting culmination to a long musical career. It reached No. 4 in the country listings and impacted the pop charts at the same time. When Cash died shortly after its release, tributes poured in from such diverse luminaries as Al Gore, Bob Dylan, Bono and Emmylou Harris. Glen Campbell said, 'I don't see any stars on the horizon that are like Johnny Cash. He was so unique. I miss him.'

Empty Chair

Johnny Cash's empathetic songs influenced artists and fans, both young and old, from all corners of the world. Artists from many musical genres have since attempted to imitate his unique musical style in the hope of capturing some of that old black magic. No one can hope to fill the space he left in country music and the wider musical world, but at least a little of the man himself lives on in his recordings and songs.

'I LOVE THE ROAD. I LOVE BEING A GYPSY.'
JOHNNY CASH

THE MAN IN BLACK

'JOHNNY CASH'S VOICE WILL ALWAYS SIGNIFY PAIN AND ENTRAPMENT AND STRUGGLE, THE SONIC EQUIVALENT OF THE BLACK GARMENTS HE ALWAYS WORE.'
AERON FOX, MUSICOLOGIST AND AUTHOR

Johnny Cash was full of contradictions. He was a staunch Republican who played for and met many presidents of the USA, and reflected in his 1997 autobiography, 'All the presidents I've known have had a lot of personal charm.' He once famously said, 'If you're not going to support the president, get out of my way so I can stand behind him.'

He performed for Richard Nixon at the White House in 1970, supporting the president's stance in the Vietnam War, but at the same time championed the individual's right to protest against it. His song 'The Man In Black' mourned the number of men being lost to the war each week.

'IT WAS ALWAYS ABOUT THE SONGS. IT DIDN'T MATTER WHO WROTE THEM, JUST HOW THE WORDS SOUNDED WHEN JOHNNY SANG THEM AND THE BELIEVABILITY.'
RICK RUBIN, PRODUCER

'AN HONEST
GUY WHO
WAS ALWAYS
SEEKING
OUT HIS
OWN
TRUTH
AND LIVING
IN HIS
OWN PAIN...'
ROSANNE
CASH,
DAUGHTER

I Walk The Line

A year after Cash's death, the Republican Party held a celebration of his life and work, yet somehow he always stood for the working class hero. Sometimes critical of the war in Iraq, he still refused to be pinned down on his political views, managing to appeal to both the landowners and the dispossessed.

His personal life became a mess of his own making. He battled an amphetamine habit on a daily basis, sometimes getting prescriptions from a dozen doctors in one week to ensure his supply. He left his first wife for June Carter who, when they first met, was married to his friend Carl Smith. 'I've always felt there's a war going on inside of me ... good fighting against evil,' he said. His less-than-perfect character struck chords with many of his listeners, who could recognize themselves in his work.

The Vanishing Race

Cash often identified with the plight of the Native Americans, such as on the album *Bitter Tears* (1964), but he also glorified cowboy mythology on *Johnny Cash Sings The Ballads Of The True West*, released the following year. He once claimed to be descended from the Cherokee tribe, but later admitted this was not true. He nonetheless won the admiration of many Native Americans for his support through music.

'Rosalynn and I so appreciate your efforts in trying to change your schedule to be with us last night. It was a wonderful evening and we missed you. Thank you for being a good and loyal friend. Sincerely, Jimmy.'

Letter from President Jimmy Carter, 8 December 1977

On *Bitter Tears*, he worked with folk musician Peter La Farge (who claimed to be descended from the Narragansett Indian tribe), and 'The Ballad Of Ira Hayes' referred to the largely forgotten Native American who raised the flag at Iwo Jima.

Come Along And Ride This Train

Cash's upbringing beside railway tracks and cotton fields inspired many of his songs. His first song, 'Hey, Porter' (1955) as well as 'Blue Train' (1962) and 'Riding On The Cotton Belt' from album *The Last Gunfighter Ballad* (1977), hark back to the days of his daddy 'riding the rods'. In 1969, he even wrote a song called 'I've Got A Thing About Trains'.

The *Blood, Sweat and Tears* album (1963) saw Cash celebrating the working man. Traditional songs from the blues tradition such as 'Tell Him I'm Gone' and 'Another Man Done Gone' lament the persecution of men working on the chain gang. On these, along with Merle Travis's 'Nine Pound Hammer' and Jimmie Rodgers' 'Waiting For A Train', Cash gave a voice to sharecroppers, cotton pickers, hobos and convicts; though he wrote songs about and performed in prisons, and was arrested seven times for public disorder, drinkand drug-related offences, he never had to serve a prison sentence.

Johnny Cash had a limited vocal range, yet had the knack of conveying sympathy and suffering through intonation. His low, gravelly voice managed to encapsulate the world of the poor, the downtrodden and the oppressed.

WALKING
THE LINE

‘I WAS
DEEPLY
INTO FOLK
MUSIC IN
THE EARLY
1960S.’
JOHNNY CASH

Johnny was brought up on the music of the legendary Carter Family, whose country/folk radio broadcasts were an inspiration. (This would have later significance when Cash met future second wife, June Carter. Her mother, Maybelle, led this popular country singing group with which June would sing from the age of ten, laying the foundations for June and Johnny's later musical and romantic partnership.) Another early influence was Leadbelly, the folk-blues pioneer whose song 'Goodnight Irene' he covered in 1957. Cash also admired the work of Hank Williams and, at home, religion was omnipresent, with gospel hymns sung around the fire. No wonder Cash developed a musical style all his own – sometimes country and gospel, other times folk and rock'n'roll.

As the only person to be inducted into the Country Music Hall of Fame, the Rock and Roll Hall of Fame and the Songwriters Hall of Fame, he represented all these American musical styles in one package.

Country Boy

Johnny Cash had a stereotypical 'country' background: the poor farmstead, sitting by the fishing hole, pickin' cotton; a heady mix of violence, drunkenness and religion in his home life; unemployment, riding the boxcars and pickin' the guitar on the front porch. Country was where he started, but as Kris Kristofferson said, 'His television show [*The Johnny Cash Show* which aired on ABC from 1969 to 1971] was really important … he brought in a lot of people who weren't normally in Nashville, like Joni Mitchell, Linda Ronstadt, James Taylor, Ray Charles...'. Cash's style of country reached out and brought everything else into it.

'Of course, I knew of him before he ever heard of me. In '55 or '56, "I Walk The Line" played all summer on the radio, and it was different than anything else you had ever heard.'

Bob Dylan

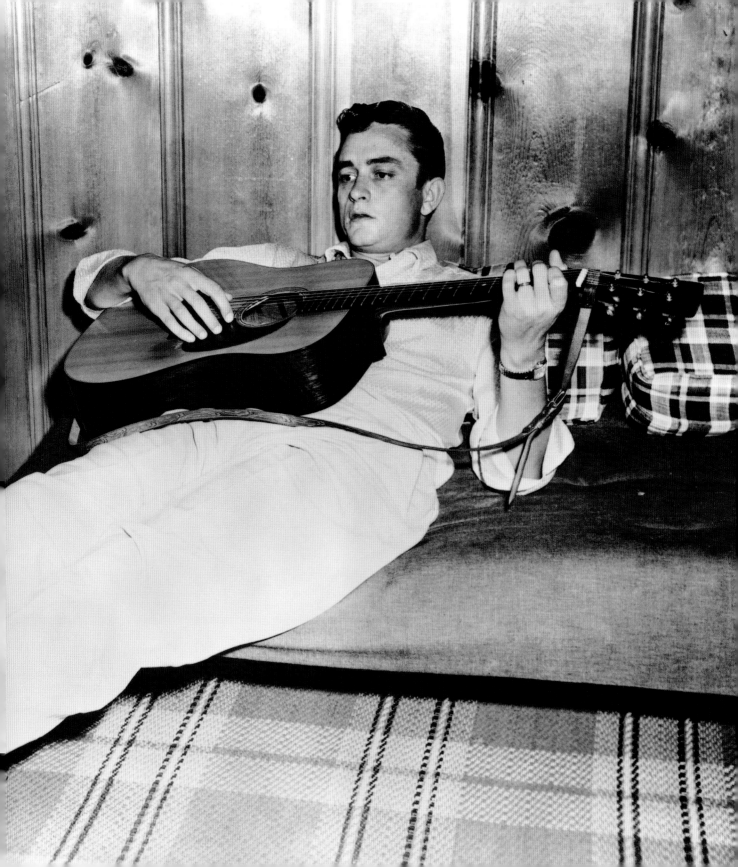

I Talk To Jesus Every Day

Gospel was there on his front porch, and as a committed Christian since he was a boy, Cash longed to make a religious album. Sam Phillips of Sun Records, the first record label to sign him, was reluctant, but Cash got his way later at Columbia when he was able to release an album of hymns with a country feel.

Song To Woody

Cash's 1959 *Songs Of Our Soil* launched him alongside folk revival giants Bob Dylan and Joan Baez. It contained folk ballads that dealt with different facets of American life, often with a mortality theme. Cash continued his move towards folk when he appeared at the first New York Folk Festival in 1965. His album *Orange Blossom Special* was hailed as a groundbreaking fusion of country and western and folk songs and included 'It Ain't Me Babe' and two more Dylan tunes.

I Will Rock And Roll With You

Although Johnny was never mainstream rock'n'roll like his Sun Records stable mate Jerry Lee Lewis, the energy and rawness of rock'n'roll rubbed off on him, particularly when playing with Carl Perkins. Cash could turn his voice to many styles of music and probably said it best in his song of the same title: 'Baby, I will rock and roll with you … if I have to.'

'JOHN, ELVIS AND THEM WERE ROCKABILLY; I WAS ROCK'N'ROLL. BUT WE ALL HAD COUNTRY IN US.'
JERRY LEE LEWIS

PULL DOWN

LETTERS

E

Rockabilly, which combines country and blues-influenced rock'n'roll, is unmistakably southern US in origin. Cash had his own take on this style – and indeed his 64th album was called *Rockabilly Blues*. Early Sun recordings such as 'Get Rhythm' or 'Hey Porter' in particular merged country and rock'n'roll into music that could simply be called Cash rockabilly.

Further On Up The Road

Cash has been acknowledged as an influence by many later singers, including Bob Dylan, Bono and Nick Cave. When they met at the 1964 Newport Folk Festival, Cash gave Dylan his guitar as a gesture of respect, and in 1969, the pair recorded more than a dozen duets together.

Many artists have covered Cash's songs: from Elvis Costello with 'Cry, Cry, Cry', Ryan Adams' 'I Still Miss Someone' to Bruce Springsteen's 'Give My Love To Rose'. His songs are as enduring as his style.

'He made a giant contribution to music, not just country style.'

Ray Charles

COTTON PICKIN' HANDS

'THERE'S NEVER BEEN TWO MONTHS GONE BY THAT I HAVEN'T DREAMED ABOUT HIM [JACK]. HE'S TRIED TO HELP TURN ME TO THE CHRISTIAN WAY OF LIFE.'

JOHNNY CASH

So many of the great voices that sang out across America during the twentieth century were born of immigrant stock. Migrants from cultures as diverse as Ireland and West Africa had both poverty and a strong singing heritage in common. Johnny Cash's family history stretches back to Scotland, with his ancestors coming to the Americas as pilgrims sailing from Glasgow in 1667. Settling first in Massachusetts, they moved south, first to Virginia and then on to Georgia, where they planted cotton and fought on the losing side in the Civil War.

Praise The Lord And Pass The Soup

Cash's grandfather became a travelling preacher who frequently took payment in food and drink for his family.

'I'M A FAIR TO MIDDLIN' MAN, AND THESE ARE COTTON PICKIN' HANDS.'

JOHNNY CASH AND JUNE CARTER CASH, 'COTTON PICKIN' HANDS'

Johnny himself was born during the Great Depression, to Ray and Carrie Rivers Cash in Kingsland, Arkansas on 26 February 1932. The child who would become Johnny Cash began life as plain JR, a boy with no first name and the middle of seven children. They lived on the side of the railroad track, and his father took work wherever he could – in a sawmill, on the railroad, or hunting to feed the kids. Sometimes he would 'ride the rods' towards potential employment – a dangerous trick, but one where he could roll off the boxcar into their own yard.

Mississippi Delta Land

Late in 1934, Ray Cash took advantage of a US government scheme that resettled destitute farmers on 20 acres of land. For no downpayment, they received a home, outbuildings, a mule and a cow, and enough food to keep them until the first crop. The first song Johnny remembered singing was 'I Am Bound For The Promised Land', sitting on the wagon heading for his new home in Dyess, Mississippi County.

The family cleared the land, and it initially produced first-quality Strict High Middlin' cotton, but as they were unable to afford fertilizer, the crop deteriorated to Fair To Middlin' quality, as immortalized in the Cash/Carter song 'Cotton Pickin' Hands'. From the age of eight, JR picked cotton with his family, working from first light to evening, when they would all drop from exhaustion. Singing was a relief from the hard work, and this upbringing would inspire his songs.

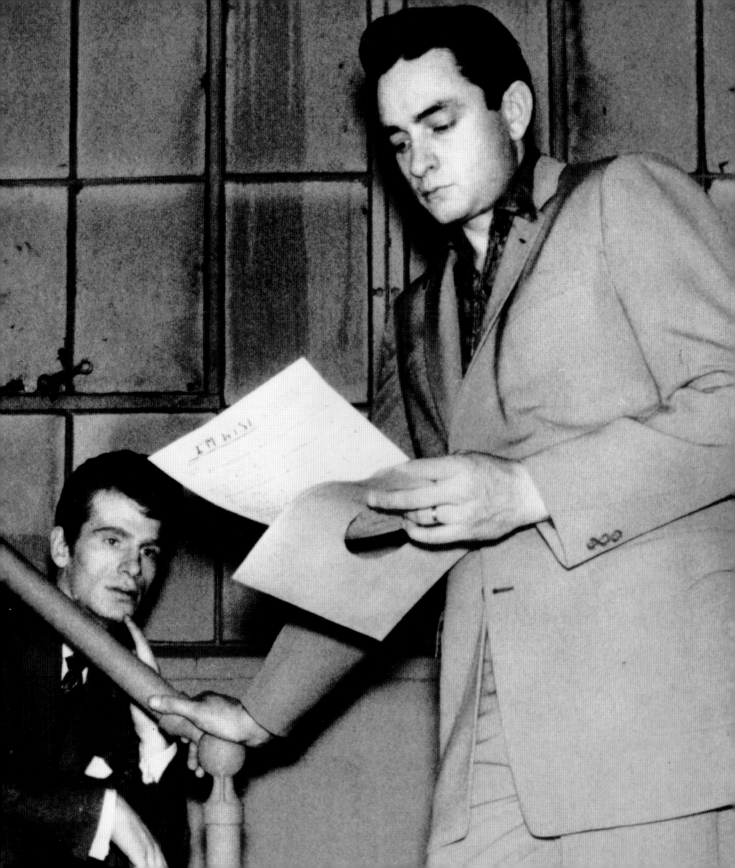

'MY SONG "FIVE FEET HIGH AND RISING" CAME FROM MY OWN EXPERIENCE [OF THE MISSISSIPPI]'.
JOHNNY CASH

THE FIRST SONG I REMEMBER SINGING WAS "I AM BOUND FOR THE PROMISED LAND".

JOHNNY CASH.

Meet Me In Heaven

JR was close to his siblings, but tragedy struck in 1943 when his older brother Jack suffered a terrible accident while cutting wood. Sliced through the middle by a power saw, he was slow to die and the family gathered around his hospital bed to sing hymns. 'Peace In The Valley', 'I'll Fly Away' and 'How Beautiful Heaven Must Be' were sung at the funeral, and all these later entered Cash's gospel repertoire.

Let There Be Country

Cash grew up listening to a wide variety of music – traditional songs, old-time ballads, country, blues and gospel (through his mother's adherence to the Pentecostal Church of God). The early religious conviction in his family would leave Johnny a committed Christian all his life.

Most of all, Cash loved country and western music on radio shows such as Smilin' Eddie Hill's *High Noon Round-Up* from WMPS/Memphis. The first song he remembered hearing was 'Hobo Bill's Last Ride' by Jimmie Rodgers. *Grand Ole Opry* broadcasts brightened his Friday and Saturday nights, and featured musicians such as Ernest Tubb, Roy Acuff and Hank Williams, who Cash idolized and would later record a tribute to.

THE SOUND OF CASH

'THE JOHNNY CASH SOUND WAS CREATED BY THE THREE OF THEM EQUALLY, YOU KNOW WHAT I MEAN? THERE WAS NONE OF THAT "BOOM CHICKA BOOM" WITHOUT MARSHALL.'
ROSANNE CASH, DAUGHTER

A distinctive bass-baritone, pick-and-strum guitar style and a mixture of dry humour and pathos in his songs made Johnny Cash unique not only in country but in music as a whole.

When he began singing as a teenager, Cash had a high tenor voice. Then, 'Suddenly my voice dropped and I was singing bomm – buh-buh – bomm, way down low in the key of E. And my mother said, "Who is that singing?" She came out of the back door and there I was…'.

Cash's mother, Carrie, played guitar and fiddle, and hers was the first voice he heard singing. She paid for him to have singing lessons, taking in washing to make the three dollars each they cost. After the third lesson, his teacher said he should have no more, and advised him

'A JOHNNY CASH RECORD WITHOUT LUTHER PERKINS ON IT WAS ONLY HALF A CASH RECORD.'
MARTY STUART, MUSICIAN

not to change the natural way he sang. He missed the teacher – a 'young, kind and very pretty' woman – more than the lessons, but later regretted not learning how to look after his voice rather than abusing it with amphetamines. He described it as a God-given gift of which he was 'the bearer, not the owner'.

Home Of The Blues

In the 1950s, Cash enjoyed listening to contemporary country and blues music, and used to visit Home Of The Blues, a record store where he bought *Blues In The Mississippi Night*, an Alan Lomax anthology of delta blues. One of his 1957 songs written for Sun Records took its name from the record shop.

His eclectic taste in music established itself early. He listened to Dewey Phillips' WHBQ show *Red, Hot And Blue*, which crossed genres and played gospel, pop, hillbilly, blues and country, with no respect for musical or racial boundaries.

Country Boy

Cash began playing guitar at the age of 12. He learnt his first chords from his mother and his childhood friend, Pete 'Jesse' Barnhill, who had adopted an unusual style, as polio during childhood had given him a withered playing hand. Maybe this influenced Johnny's distinctive playing.

'MAN, YOU'RE TALKING ABOUT A CLASSIC SOUND! THERE'S NOT ANOTHER ONE LIKE IT. I MEAN, THERE'S VAMPS AND THERE'S VAMPS, BUT THERE ISN'T THAT SOUND.' SAM PHILLIPS, OWNER OF SUN RECORDS

'I REMEMBER TUNING IN ALL KINDS OF POP MUSIC – BING CROSBY, THE ANDREWS SISTERS – AND GOSPEL AND BLUES.'

JOHNNY CASH

In Memphis, his brother Roy introduced him to Marshall Grant and Luther Perkins, guitar players who shared Cash's love for hillbilly music. Four guitar players (including AW 'Red' Kernodle) jammed together, and the result was a muddle. Grant perceptively said to Perkins and Cash, 'Somebody's gotta learn how to play lead guitar and somebody's gotta learn how to play bass if we expect to have any success like Elvis has had.'

Luther Played The Boogie

Luther borrowed an electric Fender Telecaster which had its volume control stuck at maximum. This led him to start muting the three bass strings (E, A and D) with the heel of his right hand, in the style of Merle Travis, and scratching a rhythm pattern. This would become an integral part of the Cash band sound.

Grant wasn't trained on the bass, but his contribution to their sound eventually proved as essential as it was rudimentary. None of the trio was a skilled musician, but their combined limitations helped create an instantly identifiable sound. 'So many people think we took ten years creating this style,' Grant later explained. 'It was there in the first eight bars [of music] we played, and we spent the next four years trying to get rid of it.'

ON AIR

'I BOUGHT
MY OWN
FIRST GUITAR
[IN GERMANY]
FOR TWENTY
DEUTSCHMARKS.'
JOHNNY CASH

After graduating from high school in 1950, Cash spent a brief period working in the Fisher automotive plant in Pontiac, Michigan before enlisting in the US Air Force. He met his future wife Vivian at a skating rink in San Antonio, where he was training for the military at Brooks Air Force Base.

At the outset of the Korean War, Cash was posted to Landsberg in Germany. He found himself working as a Morse code and radio operator.

He discovered that when you signed up for the USAF, you couldn't have only initials for a first name, and at this point he adopted John R. Cash as his legal name.

'WE'D SIT
AROUND
TOGETHER
IN THE
BARRACKS
AND
MURDER
THE
COUNTRY
SONGS OF
THE DAY.'
JOHNNY
CASH

'THE EXTENT OF MY DREAM WAS TO SING ON THE RADIO STATION IN MEMPHIS.'

JOHNNY CASH

I Was There When It Happened

Cash's job was with the USAF Security Service, intercepting Soviet radio communications. He was the first man outside Russia to learn of Stalin's death, and later tracked the first Soviet jet-powered bomber's flight from Moscow to Smolensk.

Because of the time difference, he could also use his radio equipment to tune into the Grand Ole Opry on Sunday mornings while it was being transmitted in the States on a Saturday night.

Belshazzar

In Germany, Cash used the time to see Europe – London, Paris and Barcelona – and turned his attention towards music. He formed the Landsberg Barbarians, which provided him with a chance to perform live, practise guitar, and start writing songs. Legend has it he accidentally played a tape of his four-piece group backwards and that the resulting drone surfaced later in 'I Walk the Line'.

Among the titles he penned around that time were 'Belshazzar', a gospel song he later described as 'the first song I wrote that I intended to record', and 'Folsom Prison Blues'. The latter was inspired by a movie he saw at the base, *Inside The Walls Of Folsom Prison* (1951), and contained probably his most famous ever line: 'I shot a man in Reno just to watch him die.'

Home Sweet Home

Discharged from the Air Force in 1954 with the rank of sergeant, Cash briefly considered joining the police, but ended up working as an appliance salesman for the Home Equipment Company. His boss there, George Bates, saw he was no salesman but, over time, advanced him over a thousand dollars (later repaid) to help get his music career off the ground.

Cash also met up again with Vivian, following a long and romantic correspondence while they were apart. Within three weeks, the couple decided to get engaged and they later married in her hometown on 7 August 1954. The ceremony, held at St Ann's Catholic Church, was performed by Vivian's uncle, Father Vincent Liberto. Cash then headed to Memphis, Tennessee, with his new wife.

Going To Memphis

Marshall Grant and Luther Perkins joined forces with Cash, and they rode about looking for gigs and performing a mainly gospel set, including the aforementioned 'Belshazzar'. Their first public performance was at a church in North Memphis, and the band – still with no name and having no stage clothes – decided on a uniform of blue jeans and black shirts.

At that stage, Cash's musical ambitions were relatively modest. He hoped only to get radio appearances around Memphis as a musician, and also fancied himself as a radio announcer. Things were about to change in a big way.

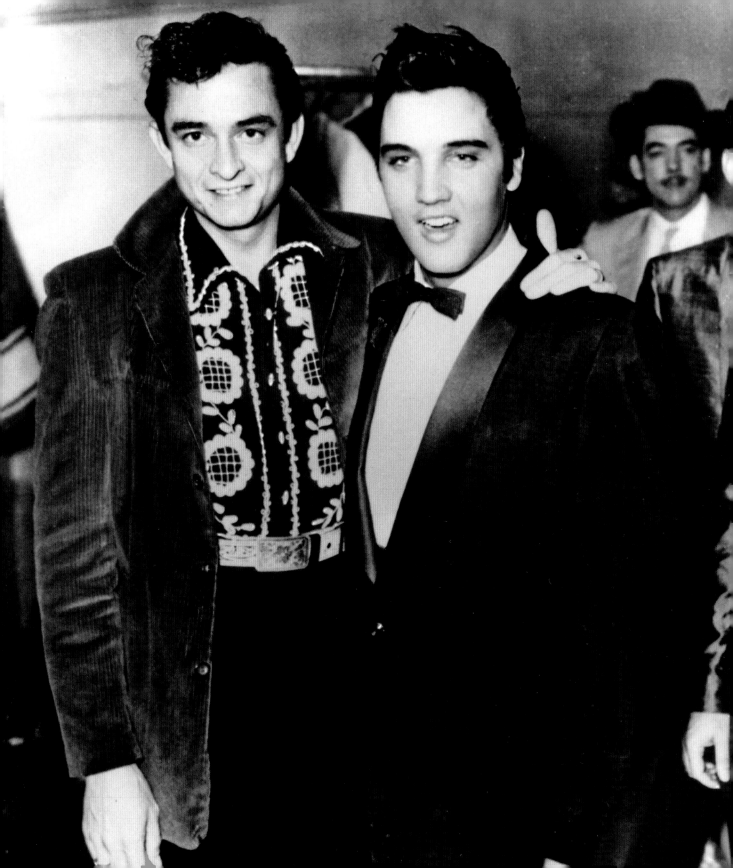

DAYS IN THE SUN

'ELVIS WAS ALREADY MAKING A NOISE IN MEMPHIS WHEN I GOT THERE IN '54.'
JOHNNY CASH

Sun Records was putting out innovative records by Elvis Presley and Carl Perkins, and Cash tried to catch label owner Sam Phillips' attention. The first time they spoke on the telephone, he introduced himself as a gospel singer. 'Sam said, "We can't sell gospel records",' he later recalled. A couple of weeks later, he called again, saying he was a country singer. Rebuffed again, he sat on Sun's doorstep until Sam let him in.

His persistence paid off. He sang his own 'I Was There When It Happened' and 'Belshazzar', plus songs by other people such as the Carter Family and Jimmie Rodgers, but Sam kept asking him, 'But what else have you written?' In the end, he performed 'Hey, Porter', at which point Sam told him to come back with his musicians in the morning.

If The Good Lord's Willing

The next day, they recorded 'Hey, Porter' and Sam told him he needed a song for the B-side. A few weeks later, he had written 'Cry, Cry, Cry' and, after 35 takes, their first single was born. Issued as Sun 221, it edged out Elvis Presley and Johnny's early heroes the Louvin Brothers to make the local No. 1 spot and No. 14 on *Billboard's* country chart.

He released two LPs on the Sun label, *Johnny Cash With His Hot And Blue Guitar* (1957) and *Sings The Songs That Made Him Famous* (1958). Both were a mix of his own songs, traditional ballads and songs by his early heroes.

The Songs That Made Him Famous

'I Walk The Line', released in 1956, shot to No. 1 on the country charts, and No. 20 on *Billboard*, making crossover history for Cash. But although he became Sun's most successful artist with hits like 'Folsom Prison Blues', he still wanted to record the gospel music he grew up on. This musical difference resulted in Cash leaving Sun in 1958 to join Columbia. He left behind enough material for an album called *Johnny Cash Sings Hank Williams* (1960).

Million Dollar Quartet

When Cash signed to Sun, he became a label mate of Elvis Presley, Carl Perkins and Jerry Lee Lewis, but in 1955, Phillips

'I WROTE "I WALK THE LINE" WHEN I WAS ON THE ROAD IN TEXAS IN 1956 HAVING A HARD TIME RESISTING THE TEMPTATION TO BE UNFAITHFUL.'

JOHNNY CASH

sold Elvis to RCA in order to keep the company afloat. In 1956, all four played in a spontaneous jam that would be immortalized in the Million Dollar Quartet recordings.

The quartet earned this moniker by a series of coincidences. Carl Perkins had been recording with Jerry Lee Lewis. Elvis arrived to see his old friend Carl and, as Cash was also in the studio, the four started singing gospel together. Sam Phillips pressed 'record' and called Bob Johnson, entertainment editor for the local newspaper the *Memphis Press-Scimitar*, who brought a photographer to capture the moment. The next day, Johnson coined the 'Million Dollar Quartet' phrase.

Remember Me

Johnny's daughter Rosanne was born on 24 May 1955, the first of four daughters in seven years. But Vivian recognized the threat to their marriage when she saw female fans clustering around her husband at his first big concert in August 1955, supporting Elvis. By the time they had three daughters in 1959, the writing was on the wall.

This period of Cash's life also saw the start of his drug-taking habits. What he described as taking a 'little white Benzedrine tablet scored with a cross' in 1957, which gave him 'unbelievable energy', would escalate into an addiction that came close to destroying his life.

'JOHNNY CASH COULD HAVE GONE BY THE WAYSIDE IF I HAD TRIED TO MAKE A ROCKER OUT OF HIM. JOHNNY CASH HAD FOLK ALL OVER HIM.' SAM PHILLIPS

ON FIRE

'EVERYBODY WAS WEARING RHINESTONES, ALL THOSE SPARKLY CLOTHES AND COWBOY BOOTS. I DECIDED TO WEAR A BLACK SHIRT AND PANTS AND SEE IF I COULD GET BY WITH IT. I DID AND I'VE WORN BLACK CLOTHES EVER SINCE.'

JOHNNY CASH

ash signed for Columbia in 1958 and on his first album, *The Fabulous Johnny Cash*, was joined by Luther Perkins on guitar and Marshall Grant on upright bass. The 'Tennessee Two' brought their unmistakable 'freight train' style to create the 'Johnny Cash sound'.

The single 'Frankie's Man, Johnny', reached No. 9; 'Don't Take Your Guns To Town' then topped the country charts for six weeks.

Where Did We Go Right?

Producer Don Law had signed Cash to Columbia and would produce his sessions for nine years. Cash himself would stay at Columbia for the next three decades. Columbia gave him artistic freedom. Careful not to alienate his fan base, in *Hymns*

By Johnny Cash (1959) he mixed gospel songs with a jaunty country style to produce songs that were still accessible. The opener 'It Was Jesus' is classic Cash and 'God Will' closes with a prophetic message: 'When no one understands or lends a helping hand/God will.' But the album failed to chart.

Songs Of Our Soil

The musically stripped-back *Songs Of Our Soil* (1959) contained secular subject matter; the Cash farm once being flooded by the Mississippi provided inspiration for 'Five Feet High And Rising', which reached No. 14. *Ride This Train* (1960) was one of the first concept albums. With a unique blend of narration and singing, it reflected Cash's passion for American culture.

During the Sixties, Cash made several further concept recordings, including *Blood, Sweat And Tears* (labouring songs, 1963) and *The Lure Of The Grand Canyon* (1961), where Cash provided spoken narration on the last track. *Bitter Tears* (1964) highlighted the plight of the Native Americans, while *Ballads Of The True West* (1965) was an experimental double album mixing frontier songs with spoken narration. From this period on, Cash would also increasingly be known for his dark attire.

Everyone Gets Crazy

By this time, Cash was a father of two girls (Rosanne and Kathy), and had moved his family to California. A third daughter, Cynthia (Cindy) was born in July 1959, but it was far from a

'I AM NOT
A CHRISTIAN
ARTIST,
I AM AN
ARTIST
WHO IS A
CHRISTIAN.'
JOHNNY
CASH

happy family. Vivian, a devout Catholic, was struggling to help him resist his addiction, but their marriage was not working thanks to a vicious circle of stress and drug abuse. Cash was never a violent man towards others, but the drugs caused rages that he took out on inanimate objects or on himself. In the end, tired of fighting both the drugs and Cash's growing attachment to June Carter, Vivian filed for divorce in the summer of 1966; it was granted in late 1967.

Ring Of Fire

Cash had met June Carter before, and been quite smitten, but late in 1961, Cash's manager booked June as a support act, and the following year she joined the Cash road show. The pair's relationship deepened, contributing to the end of his first marriage. In 1963, Cash recorded 'Ring Of Fire', written by June Carter and Merle Kilgore, and it became the biggest hit of his career, charting for seven weeks at No 1.

1967 was a year of mixed fortunes for the singer. Cash recorded a duet with June: 'Jackson', (with Carl Perkins on guitar) which raced to No. 2 in the charts. Later in the year, he was involved in a car crash and arrested after he was found to be carrying prescription drugs, and spent a night in jail. He also attempted (and failed) to commit suicide. June's unwavering support of him following this event cemented their relationship, and with her help he was able to face – and defeat – his demons. As he recovered from his near-death experience, 'Jackson' was nominated for (and later won) a Grammy award: it looked like Johnny Cash was not finished yet.

"RING OF FIRE"] RAISED A LOT OF EYEBROWS IN NASHVILLE BECAUSE WE USED TRUMPETS ON IT."

JOHNNY CASH

NASHVILLE YEARS

'I'M A MUSICIAN MYSELF, I'M A JAZZ ENTHUSIAST. BUT WHEN JOHNNY CASH CAME IN IT DIDN'T MATTER WHAT KIND OF MUSIC IT WAS. IT WAS A PLEASURE.'

MILLARD DEDMON, A FOLSOM PRISONER IN 1968

Johnny and June were married on 1 March 1968 at a church in Franklin, Kentucky. June wore light blue and carried a bouquet of red roses, while Johnny sported a black suit and a red rose on his lapel. Even before they were married, Cash and Carter had won a Grammy for Best C&W Performance by a Duo/Group for 'Jackson'.

Second Honeymoon

June had been married and divorced twice, first to actor and composer Carl Smith and then to Edwin L. Nix. There are seven Carter/Cash children: Rosanne (1955), Carlene (1955, daughter of June and Carl Smith), Kathleen (1956), Rosie (1958–2003, daughter of June and Edwin Nix), Cindy (1959) and Tara (1961). John Carter Cash (1970) is Johnny and June's only child.

Daddy Sang Bass

In 1968, 'Daddy Sang Bass', with writer Carl Perkins on guitar, reached No. 1 for six weeks. It was taken from *The Holy Land*, an album of songs about Israel that were inspired by a visit. It was also in 1968 that Bob Wootton joined Cash's backing band after the tragic death of long-serving guitarist Luther Perkins in a house fire. According to Cash, Wootton '... came as close as any man could to filling the hole Luther had left'.

Folsom Prison Blues

Cash had been playing in prisons almost ever since writing 'Folsom Prison Blues'; inmates would write to Cash asking him to play. His first prison performance was at Huntsville State Prison in 1957, and in January 1968, he recorded two shows at Folsom itself. Released by Columbia as *At Folsom Prison* (1968), his first LP with producer Bob Johnston hit No. 1 in the country charts.

A further concert at San Quentin Prison in 1969 yielded the crossover hit single 'A Boy Named Sue', a novelty song written by Shel Silverstein. It reached No. 1 on the country charts and No. 2 on the US pop Top 10.

Singin' In Vietnam Talkin' Blues

The spring of 1969 saw Johnny and June make a pilgrimage to Vietnam. Cash was appalled by what he saw and the tales he

'THAT'S A GOOD STORY. WOMAN [JUNE] RESCUES MAN FROM THE ABYSS... THE TRUTH IS MY DAD STRUGGLED WITH ADDICTION FOR THE REST OF HIS LIFE.'

ROSANNE CASH, DAUGHTER

heard about the war. The couple played music at night and visited field hospitals during the day. The experience affected them greatly, and would inspire songs like 'Man In Black'.

In 1969, Bob Dylan was recording for Columbia, also with Bob Johnston as producer. Cash duetted on 'Girl From The North Country' and contributed sleeve notes to Dylan's *Nashville Skyline* LP. Like Dylan, Cash was inspired by the social consciousness of the time, and particularly the Vietnam War, so they had a common cause.

Cash ended 1969 with no fewer than nine albums in the *Billboard* charts. But this would be the end of the glory days for many years.

To Beat The Devil

Between 1969 and 1971, *The Johnny Cash Show* was broadcast on the ABC network, and showcased guests who influenced him, from Ray Charles and Louis Armstrong to contemporary performers such as Joni Mitchell and Linda Ronstadt. Artists who received a career boost from the show included Kenny Rogers, James Taylor, Derek and the Dominos and Kris Kristofferson.

Cash released *Hello, I'm Johnny Cash* (1970), on which he covered his first Kristofferson song, 'To Beat The Devil', and the soundtrack album to the eponymous film *I Walk The Line* (1970), starring Gregory Peck. 'Flesh And Blood' from this album became another No. 1 country hit.

'I FIRST HEARD OF [JOHNNY] THROUGH ELVIS PRESLEY. ELVIS WOULD MAKE ME GO INTO THESE LITTLE CAFES AND LISTEN TO JOHN [ON THE JUKEBOX].'
JUNE CARTER CASH

GOSPEL ROAD

'JOHNNY CASH WAS NOT ONLY A LEGEND, BUT WAS A CLOSE PERSONAL FRIEND. JOHNNY WAS A GOOD MAN WHO ALSO STRUGGLED WITH MANY CHALLENGES IN HIS LIFE. JOHNNY WAS A DEEPLY RELIGIOUS MAN.'
BILLY GRAHAM, EVANGELIST

Early in 1970, 'If I Were A Carpenter', a Tim Hardin song and duet between Johnny and June from *Hello, I'm Johnny Cash*, rose to No. 2 in the country charts. The 1970 Grammys saw Johnny collect two awards: Best Country Vocal Performance, Male, for 'A Boy Named Sue', and Best Album Notes for Bob Dylan's *Nashville Skyline* album sleeve. 'If I Were A Carpenter' went on to win a Grammy for Best Country Performance by a Duo/Group in 1971; it would be Cash's last such recognition for more than 15 years.

May 1971 saw the final broadcast of *The Johnny Cash Show*, which had continued to feature names such as Neil Young and Gordon Lightfoot, though it briefly returned to the small screen in 1976 on CBS-TV.

'A MAN WHO REALLY HELPED ME DEAL WITH MY FAITH AS A PUBLIC PERSON IN THE SECULAR WORLD WAS BILLY GRAHAM.'
JOHNNY CASH

WHEN HE WENT TO VIETNAM IT REALLY HIT HIM – IT REALLY GOT TO HIM.'

KATHY CASH, DAUGHTER

The Devil's Right Hand

The 1970 Kent State shootings, in which the National Guard killed four unarmed students, were followed by widespread demonstrations over the Vietnam War and other social issues. 'Man In Black', Cash's ultimate protest song, suddenly appealed to a much wider audience than before. Johnny Cash now officially became 'The Man In Black' with the single hitting the No. 2 position. The album of the same name, released in May 1971, also included the political 'Singin' In Vietnam Talkin' Blues', yet started with a duet with evangelist Billy Graham, 'The Preacher Said Jesus Said'.

Taking To The Small Screen

In 1971, he toured Europe with a complete Johnny Cash stage show – the Tennessee Three, the Carter Family, the Statler Brothers and Carl Perkins. He appeared on television in Denmark and in the UK, where his records were selling in greater numbers than at home. 'A Thing Called Love', on which he was backed by the Evangel Temple Choir, made No. 4 as a single and the album (also called *A Thing Called Love*) made No. 8 in the UK, while the album stalled at No. 112 on the *Billboard* listing. Much of 1972 was also spent touring Europe.

Cash starred alongside Kirk Douglas in the western *A Gunfight* (1971), and in March 1972, he made a guest appearance on TV detective show *Columbo*. Another small-screen appearance found him singing 'Five Feet High And Rising' on *Sesame Street*. The character Biff, with whom he shared the

screen, stacked symbolic foot-high blocks, but the song ended not with drowned bodies but with Cash advising children to learn how to swim.

At The Wailing Wall

In May 1971, Johnny and June set off again for the Holy Land to film and record *Gospel Road*, a documentary-style narration of the life of Jesus with Cash as narrator and June playing Mary Magdalene, although it would not be released until 1973. It was also in 1971 that Cash acquired what became his trademark Martin D-28 guitar, known as The Bon Aqua after his 100-acre farm in Tennessee. Returning from touring, Johnny would go there alone, 'to cook my own food, read my own books, tend my own garden, water my own land, and think, write, compose, rest, and reflect in peace.'

The end of 1971 brought *The Johnny Cash Collection*, a second volume of greatest hits, which would become his last platinum album for some years. *America (A 200-Year Salute In Story And Song)*, another concept LP with narrative interwoven between new and previously issued 'period' songs, was released in 1972. The album reached No. 3 in the country charts, but did not cross over into the US pop charts.

'He had a really radical TV show ... to be endorsed by someone like Cash was really something, like being endorsed by Dylan.'
Kris Kristofferson

SILVER
PIECES

'ONE THING
I'VE LEARNED
ABOUT
JOHNNY CASH
IS THAT
YOU DON'T
TELL HIM
WHAT
TO SING.'
RICHARD NIXON

The film *Gospel Road* was finally released in 1973, the same year that Cash shared a stage with evangelist Billy Graham and British pop idol Cliff Richard at London's Wembley Stadium. Acknowledging his religion in a public fashion was an important element of his life.

Neither the soundtrack, with music by Kris Kristofferson, Cash, and other songwriters, nor the film was a commercial success, although film screenings on college campuses were sponsored by Campus Crusade for Christ over the next two decades.

Cash released a prison album with a difference in 1973. *På Österåker* (At Österåker) was recorded at the Österåker Prison in Sweden the previous October.

'I HAD THIS IDEA FOR A SONG, HAD THE FIRST VERSE, AND I STAYED UP ALL NIGHT THINKING, "OH, I CAN PLAY THIS FOR [CASH]".'

NICK LOWE, SON-IN-LAW

'YOU'VE GOT A SONG YOU'RE SINGING FROM YOUR GUT, YOU WANT THAT AUDIENCE TO FEEL IT IN THEIR GUT... THEŸ'VE GOT TO BE ABLE TO RELATE TO WHAT YOU'RE DOING.'
JOHNNY CASH

One Piece At A Time

Cash's first autobiography, inevitably titled *The Man In Black*, wa
published in 1975, and the following year, the album *One Piece
At A Time*, on which he shared billing with the Tennessee Three
(including drummer W. S. Holland), would prove his biggest in
four years thanks to the success of the title song.

A song by country singer Wayne Kemp, 'One Piece
At A Time' describes a worker in a car plant building his own
vehicle from smuggled stolen parts. A surprise novelty hit, i
became Cash's last country Top 40 single to make both the US
and UK pop charts.

In the same year, he also released an album of child-centred
songs, *The Johnny Cash Children's Album*.

Sold Out Of Flag Poles

The United States' bicentennial year was in 1976, and Johnny
Cash, after a concert at the Washington Monument, came off
stage to ring a replica of the Liberty Bell in front of the crowd
as red, white and blue fireworks filled the sky. Cash maintained
his reputation as a friend of presidents when Jimmy Carter
served from 1977 to 1981. A distant relation through June,
Carter gave the Cashes their third presidential tour of the
White House.

The American Music Awards honoured Johnny with its
special Award of Merit in January 1977. He continued to

'I HAVE NEVER KNOWN A GREATER MAN AMONG MEN.'

JOHNNY CASH [OF BILLY GRAHAM]

release two albums or more a year: late Seventies' output included *The Last Gunfighter Ballad*, *The Rambler*, with singles 'Lady' and 'After The Ball', *Gone Girl* and *I Would Like To See You Again*. All hovered around the No. 30 position in the country charts.

When asked about his proudest achievement in music, Cash later nominated his election to the Nashville Songwriters Hall of Fame in 1977 as 'the big one, the one that meant the most … to recognize a talent that comes from God through a person.'

A Believer Sings The Truth

A British tour to promote the Seventies' last album *Silver* took place in March 1979, with a cast including the Carter Family and the Tennessee Trumpets. Cash released a gospel double album *A Believer Sings The Truth* (1979) before starting work on *Rockabilly Blues*. This contained a single, 'Without Love', written and produced in London by Nick Lowe, who had just married Cash's stepdaughter Carlene Carter. The album also featured Carl Perkins-influenced guitarist Dave Edmunds.

Communication and empathy with his audience was Cash's watchword from the outset. He made a point of keeping his songs real: 'It's like a novelist writing far-out things. If it makes a point and makes sense, then people like to read that. But if it's off in left-field and goes over the edge, you lose it.'

MUSICAL OUTLAW

'IN THE
1980S I WAS
INVISIBLE
IN THE
CHARTS.'
JOHNNY CASH

T he 1980s started well. Cash was inducted into the Country Music Hall of Fame, the youngest living inductee at age 48.

April 1981 saw Carl Perkins and Jerry Lee Lewis join him in Stuttgart, Germany, and their performance was released by Columbia as *The Survivors Live*. Highlights included Cash's 'Get Rhythm' and Perkins' 'Blue Suede Shoes'; they would collaborate again on *Class Of '55*, with Roy Orbison, in 1985.

Cash continued his television career with an episode of *Little House On The Prairie*, with wife June, and played John Brown in the 1985 American Civil War mini series *North And South*.

Up And Down

The 1980s were the slowest period of Cash's record-selling career. Albums *Rockabilly Blues* (1980), *The Adventures Of Johnny Cash* (1982), *Johnny 99* (1983, and including covers of two Springsteen songs) and *Rainbow* (1984), made little impact, although 1981's *The Baron* entered the country Top 30 and the title track ('The Baron') was a No. 10 country hit.

Marshall Grant, who had played bass from the beginning and served as road manager for many years, left under a cloud in 1980. Lawsuits were settled out of court.

Low record sales forced Johnny and June to sell jewellery to pay their domestic staff. They were not short of real estate, though: they owned a main home on Old Hickory Lake just outside Nashville (where they opened a museum and shop – The House of Cash, run by Johnny's mother; Johnny also set up an exotic animal park there); a farm at Bon Aqua, Tennessee; a house in Port Richey, Florida and a holiday home, Cinnamon Hill, in Jamaica.

Goin' Down The Road Feelin' Bad

In the early Eighties, Johnny was attacked by an ostrich from the House of Cash exotic animal park. Broken ribs meant he had to be given morphine; this led to a near-deadly cocktail of amphetamines, alcohol and prescription painkillers, ending in a new low in 1983 when on tour in

London. Empty wine bottles from the minibar were piling up under his son's bed. Hallucinating spiders, he smashed up his hand on a wall and the resultant infection saw him admitted to hospital – where they discovered he had internal bleeding from the ostrich attack. This led to more painkillers and more hallucinations. Finally, all his friends and relations, including his son, gathered at the bedside to tell him they had had enough. Cash went into rehab.

The Highwayman

In 1985, guitarist Bob Wootton pulled out of shows due to a family emergency. Waylon Jennings filled in and he and Johnny later joined forces with Willie Nelson and Kris Kristofferson to form country supergroup the Highwaymen. The quartet's self-titled debut went to No. 1 on the country charts in 1985 and was followed by *Highwayman 2* in 1990.

Cash's Columbia recording contract was due to end in 1986, and his parting shot was the 'intentionally atrocious' 'Chicken In Black'. He signed with Mercury from 1987 to 1991, and his first album was *Johnny Cash Is Coming To Town* (1987). One of the tracks, 'The Night Hank Williams Came To Town', would become a live favourite.

Man In White

With time on his hands, Cash published his only novel, *Man In White* (1986), a fictional account of the life of Paul the Apostle.

'...IT WAS JUST NEW FACES [IN THE 1980S], WHO'S NEW AND CASH DIDN'T FIT THE FORMULA OF THE TIME.'

RICK BLACKBURN, FORMER CEO, CBS NASHVILLE

In 1988, he campaigned for Democratic presidential candidate Al Gore. Later that year, he was admitted to a Nashville hospital for open-heart surgery. In December his 75th studio album, *Water From The Wells Of Home*, was released, featuring an all-star cast including Paul McCartney, but barely scraped into the country Top 50.

You Too?

As the doldrums decade came to an end, U2's Bono sought Cash out while on an American road trip. An informal jam set the scene for further collaboration in the Nineties. The Songwriters Guild of America chose Cash as the 1989 recipient for their Aggie Award, while in 1990, the National Academy of Recording Arts & Sciences (NARAS) acknowledged him as a 'Living Legend'.

'Johnny didn't get down when people weren't buying his records in the Eighties. He'd just go down in the woods for a while, and not meet a lot of people, and get himself together.'

Glen Campbell

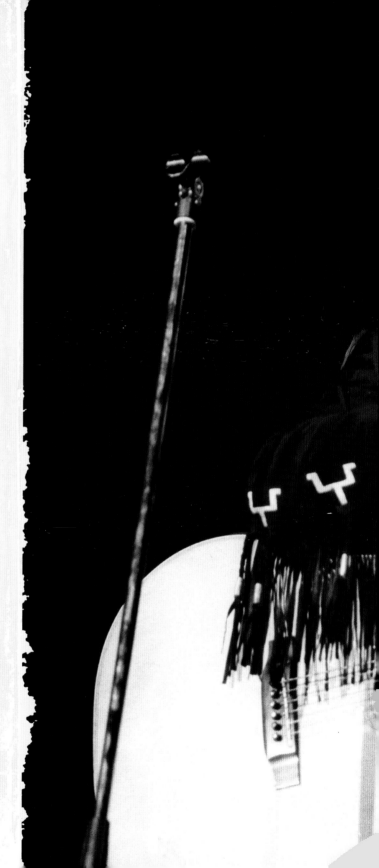

LIVING LEGEND

'HE WAS
SPELLBINDING,
BLOODY
BRILLIANT.
THAT WAS
ONE OF
MY BEST
BOOKINGS
OF ALL TIME.'
MICHAEL EAVIS,
GLASTONBURY
ORGANIZER

The 1990s started unpromisingly, with Cash and his son both undergoing spells in rehab. Johnny had managed to stay off drugs for several years, but deteriorated when he lost his mother Carrie in March 1991. The early Nineties also saw June waging her own battle with prescription drugs.

Boom Chicka Boom

Johnny opened his musical 1990s with *Boom Chicka Boom*, taking its title from the Tennessee Three's characteristic sound. In a biblical vein, he also recorded *Johnny Cash Reads The Complete New Testament*. In 1992, he was inducted into the Rock and Roll Hall of Fame, becoming one of only a handful of artists in both the rock and country halls.

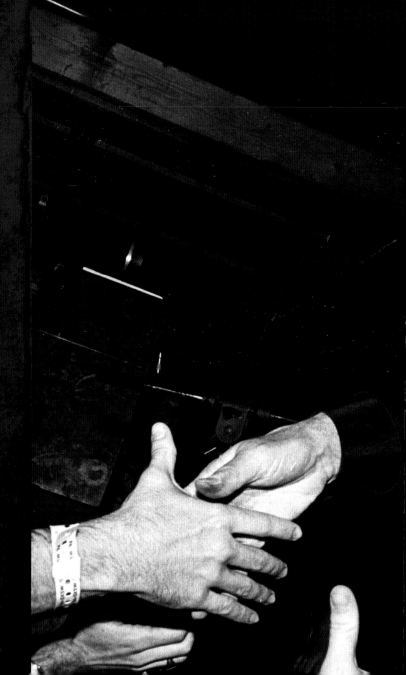

'I'VE HAD
43 YEARS OF
TOURING.
THAT'S
ENOUGH.
I CAN
DIRECT MY
ENERGIES
MORE TO
RECORDING
NOW.'
JOHNNY
CASH

The Wanderer

June and Johnny duetted on 'It Ain't Me Babe' for Bob Dylan's 30th anniversary concert in October 1992. Metal/rap producer Rick Rubin was impressed by the audience's reaction to the 62-year-old performer.

The contact made with U2 also bore fruit when Cash was playing in Dublin with Kris Kristofferson in 1993. They linked up to record 'The Wanderer' for the Irish group's *Zooropa* album, and a new audience became aware of Johnny Cash.

I'm A Newborn Man

Rick Rubin approached Cash in 1993, suggesting they 'get together … I asked him to play me songs he loves or ones he remembered from childhood.' Cash brought in 'Delia's Gone', and 'Drive On', a song from his Mercury period too good to be wasted. Songs Rubin brought included Tom Waits' 'Down There By The Train' and, notoriously, 'Thirteen', by heavy metal artist Glenn Danzig.

Cash signed to Rubin's American Recordings in 1993 and was marketed to a younger generation as a solo singer with just a guitar. He won Grammy awards (*American Recordings* (1994) – Best Contemporary Folk Album; *Unchained* (1996) – Best Country Album) from the wider music industry, but not from Nashville, which did not consider him 'country' enough to award him anything. The macabre video to accompany 'Delia's Gone', starring Kate Moss, was not aired by Country Music Television (CMT).

'HE IS PROBABLY ONE OF THE COOLEST GUYS THAT I HAVE EVER MET. HE IS A REAL MUSICIAN… HE IS A REALLY NICE GUY AND A GREAT SONGWRITER.'
GLENN DANZIG

Drive On

Cash kept busy in 1995, appearing at Britain's most prestigious music festival, Glastonbury, and was given a Grammy nomination for Best Male Country Vocal Performance for 'Rusty Cage' on *Unchained*. A third Highwaymen album, *The Road Goes On Forever*, would prove the last prior to Jennings' death in 2002.

In 1998, Cash and American Records attacked the apathy of the country music establishment by running a full-page advertisement in the music press which read: 'American Recordings and Johnny Cash would like to acknowledge the Nashville music establishment and country radio for your support', showing Cash in snarling mood at his San Quentin live prison concert.

Meet Me In Heaven

During a performance in October 1997 in Flint, Michigan, Cash revealed the road might not go on for ever due to Parkinson's disease. After nearly falling over trying to retrieve a guitar pick, he insisted bravely. 'It's all right. I refuse to give it some ground in my life.' The diagnosis was modified to diabetes, but as he approached 70, public appearances would become rare.

An album recorded in 1997, *VH1 Storytellers: Johnny Cash & Willie Nelson*, featured a duet on '(Ghost) Riders In The Sky', which made No. 25 in the country chart. Ending the Nineties on a high, Cash received a very special Grammy in 1999, The Lifetime Achievement Award, for his creative contributions of outstanding artistic significance to the field of recording.

AMERICAN MAN

'TO HEAR THAT
JOHNNY WAS
INTERESTED IN
DOING MY SONG
WAS A DEFINING
MOMENT IN MY
LIFE'S WORK. TO
HEAR THE
RESULT REALLY
REMINDED ME
HOW BEAUTIFUL,
TOUCHING AND
POWERFUL
MUSIC CAN BE.'
TRENT REZNOR,
NINE INCH NAILS

Cash started the new century in the same vein as he finished the old: in 2001, he picked up the National Medal of Arts, the USA's highest award for artistic excellence. The third album in the American Recordings series, *American III: Solitary Man*, released in October 2000, became Cash's highest-charting solo studio LP since 1976, reaching No. 11 on the country chart. It contained Tom Petty's belligerent 'I Won't Back Down', a response to his illness, while he also covered 'One' by U2. He won Best Male Country Vocal Performance for his version of Neil Diamond's 1966 song 'Solitary Man'.

'Cash represented America as Americans.'

Obituary, The Independent

Desperado

The fourth in the American Recordings series was Cash's 87th and last album of his life. Released in November 2002, *American IV: The Man Comes Around* was sparse, reflective and solo. On it, he covered songs dealing mostly with the theme of mortality – Lennon and McCartney's 'In My Life', Irish ballad 'Danny Boy' and the Eagles' 'Desperado'. It also contained 'Hurt', a song written by Trent Reznor of Nine Inch Nails, and the Grammy-winning video featured clips of him as a younger man mixed with him in 2002, frail but unbowed. This catapulted the album to No. 22 in the *Billboard* pop listing and No. 2 on the country chart. It was Cash's first non-compilation album to go gold for over 30 years, and it progressed to platinum after his death.

Despite his desire to go on working, the abuse Cash had put himself through over the years showed in the deterioration of his characteristic vocal sounds. Rick Rubin said, 'If you listen to all of the [American Recordings] albums in a row, we hear both his physical deterioration, and along with that, deeper depths of emotion in the performances. He always felt that his voice was the thing he could always rely on. When that stopped being the case, he had to find new ways to get across the material.'

Hurt

By the end of 2002, Cash's deteriorating health was causing concern. June Carter Cash had an operation to replace a

heart valve on 7 May 2003 and died eight days later, predeceasing him by four months. She was 73.

It soon became obvious Johnny could not go on without June. He refused to sleep in their bed and gave away all the furniture she had bought. He made a couple of surprise performances in her home town in Virginia, fulfilling a promise to June and reading a tribute to his wife before singing 'Ring Of Fire'. But it was clearly a struggle to get to the end of the song.

Free

On 12 September 2003, the news broke that Johnny Cash had died from respiratory complications from diabetes, aged 71. This came just days after he was released from a Tennessee hospital after being treated for a stomach ailment. While in hospital, he had had to miss the MTV Video Music Awards in New York, where the video for 'Hurt' won an award in the best cinematography category.

Cash was buried next to June in Hendersonville Memory Gardens near his home in Tennessee, and his funeral was attended by all seven children and 16 grandchildren.

'Over the years he demonstrated a broad musical perspective, never being afraid to record songs of social commentary.'

Lyle Lovett

'EVERY MAN COULD RELATE TO HIM, BUT NOBODY COULD BE HIM.'
BONO, U2

THE ROAD GOES ON FOREVER

'I HAVE ALWAYS ENJOYED BEING A PART OF HIS LIFE. I'VE ALWAYS LOVED HIM, AND HE'S ALWAYS LOVED ME.'
JUNE CARTER CASH

Johnny Cash was one of popular music's most influential artists, breaking down the barriers between rockabilly, country, pop and folk with consummate ease. Yet when 2006's *American V: A Hundred Highways* reached No. 1 in the US pop charts, it was only the second time a Johnny Cash album had achieved this (the first was *Live From San Quentin*), although he had often topped the country charts.

Out Among The Stars

Both *American V* and *American VI: Ain't No Grave* (2010) contained new recordings by Cash made in studio sessions just prior to his death. *Out Among The Stars* (2014) was a series of 'lost' sessions recorded between 1981 and 1984 with producer Billy Sherrill, and featuring duets with June and Waylon Jennings.

Redemption

The biopic *Walk The Line* was released in 2005. Directed by James Mangold, it charted Johnny Cash's rise to fame, from his early life picking cotton in Arkansas through the Sun years to his country-music classics from the end of the 1960s. It took four years for the producers to secure the rights to the story and another four to get the film made by Fox.

Johnny had approved Joaquin Phoenix to play him because he liked his performance in the movie *Gladiator* (2000), and June had also approved Reese Witherspoon for her role. *Walk The Line* went on to garner worldwide acclaim and win Witherspoon an Oscar for Best Actress.

The movie reminds us how influential Johnny Cash was in his early days. He was part of the movement that made country music more acceptable in the USA in the late 1960s, as part of a search for an authentic America.

An attempt was made to recapture more of the Cash magic with the musical *Ring Of Fire* (2006). Unfortunately, it lasted less than a month on Broadway before folding, possibly because the venue was too large. In contrast, the musical play *Million Dollar Quartet*, which immortalized the 1956 Sun sessions with Elvis, Jerry Lee Lewis and Carl Perkins,

'JOHNNY CASH HELPED ME GET OUT OF PRISON.'
DAVID ALLAN COE, MUSICIAN'

was a moderate hit, playing nearly 500 Broadway performances and transferring successfully to London's West End.

A Legend In My Time

Johnny Cash left us over 1,000 songs and many more recordings. His talent filtered through to his children; both Rosanne and John Carter Cash are notable musicians in their own right. He supported up-and-coming artists throughout his career and, although politically aware and the friend of presidents, always sided with what he felt was right.

Despite his complexities and the darker side of his addictions, Cash always bounced back. He wrote his own epitaph: 'My life has been simple: cotton as a youth and music as an adult.'

'He just knew life was hard,
and we knew that he knew.
That's why he gave hope to anyone
who ever went through a hard time...
what you saw on TV was what you
saw when the cameras turned away.'

Bob Schieffer, CBS News

FURTHER INFORMATION

VITAL INFO

Birth Name: JR Cash
Birth & Death Dates: 26 February 1932–12 September 2003
Birthplace: Kingsland, Arkansas
Nationality: American
Height: 1.87 m (6 ft 1 in)
Hair Colour: Black
Eye Colour: Brown

DISCOGRAPHY

Albums (selected)

Johnny Cash With His Hot And Blue Guitar (1957)
Sings The Songs That Made Him Famous (1958)
The Fabulous Johnny Cash (1958)
Songs Of Our Soil (1959)
Ride This Train (1960)
Ring of Fire: The Best Of Johnny Cash (1963)
Blood, Sweat And Tears (1963)
I Walk The Line (1964)
Bitter Tears: Ballads Of The American Indian (1964)
Orange Blossom Special (1965)
Sings The Ballads Of The True West (1965)
Everybody Loves A Nut (1966)
Happiness Is You (1966)
From Sea To Shining Sea (1968)
At Folsom Prison (1968)
The Holy Land (1969)
At San Quentin (1969)
Hello, I'm Johnny Cash (1970)

The Johnny Cash Show (1970)
The World Of Johnny Cash (1970)
Man In Black (1971)
A Thing Called Love (1972)
America: A 200 Year Salute In Story And Song (1972)
Any Old Wind That Blows (1973)
The Gospel Road (1973)
Ragged Old Flag (1974)
Junkie And The Juicehead Minus Me (1974)
The Johnny Cash Children's Album (1975)
Look At Them Beans (1975)
Strawberry Cake (1976)
One Piece At A Time (1976)
The Last Gunfighter Ballad (1977)
The Rambler (1977)
I Would Like To See You Again (1978)
Silver (1979)
Rockabilly Blues (1980)
The Baron (1981)
The Survivors Live (1982)
The Adventures Of Johnny Cash (1982)
Johnny Cash Is Coming To Town (1987)
Water From The Wells Of Home (1988)
Boom Chicka Boom (1990)
The Mystery of Life (1991)
American Recordings (1994)
Unchained (1996)
American III: Solitary Man (2000)
American IV: The Man Comes Around (2002)
American V: A Hundred Highways (2006)
American VI: Ain't No Grave (2010)
Out Among The Stars (2014)

Singles (selected; US Country chart position unless stated otherwise)

1955: 'So Doggone Lonesome' (US No. 4)
1956: 'I Walk The Line' (US No. 1)
       'There You Go' (US No. 1)
1957: 'Next In Line' (US No. 9)
       'Home Of The Blues' (US No. 3)

1958: 'Ballad Of A Teenage Queen' (US No. 1)
'Guess Things Happen That Way' (US No. 1)
'The Ways Of A Woman In Love' (US No. 2)
'All Over Again' (US No. 4)

1959: 'Don't Take Your Guns To Town' (US No. 1)
'Frankie's Man, Johnny' (US No. 9)
'I Got Stripes' (US No. 4)

1960: 'Seasons Of My Heart' (US No. 10)

1962: 'In The Jailhouse Now' (US No. 8)

1963: 'Ring Of Fire' (US No. 1)
'The Matador' (US No. 2)

1964: 'Understand Your Man' (US No. 1)
'The Ballad Of Ira Hayes' (US No. 3)
'It Ain't Me Babe' with June Carter Cash (US No. 4)

1965: 'Orange Blossom Special' (US No. 3)
'The Songs Of Katie Elder' (US No. 10)
'Happy To Be With You' (US No. 9)

1966: 'The One On The Right Is On The Left' (US No. 2)

1967: 'Rosanna's Going Wild' (US No. 2)
'Jackson' with June Carter Cash (US No. 2)
'Long-Legged Guitar Pickin' Man' with June Carter
Cash (US No. 6)

1968: 'Folsom Prison Blues' (live; US No. 1)
'Daddy Sang Bass' (US No. 1)

1969 'A Boy Named Sue' (US No. 1 (Country & Pop), UK No. 4)
'Blistered' (US No. 4)
'If I Were A Carpenter' with June Carter Cash (US No. 2)

1970: 'What Is Truth' (US No. 3)
'Sunday Mornin' Comin' Down' (live; US No. 1)
'Flesh And Blood' (US No. 1)

1971: 'Man In Black' (US No. 3)
'A Thing Called Love' (US No. 2, UK No. 4 (Pop))

1972: 'Kate' (US No. 2)
'Oney' (US No. 2)
'Any Old Wind That Blows' (US No. 3)

1976: 'One Piece At A Time' (US No. 1)

1978 'There Ain't No Good Chain Gang' with Waylon
Jennings (US No. 2)

1979: '(Ghost) Riders In The Sky' (US No. 2)

AWARDS (SELECTED)

Academy of Country Music
1985: Single of the Year ('Highwayman')

Americana Music Association
2002: 'Spirit of Americana' Free Speech Award
2003: Album of the Year (*American IV: The Man Comes Around*)
Artist of the Year

Country Music Association
1968: Album of the Year (*At Folsom Prison*)
1969: Album of the Year (*At San Quentin*)
Entertainer of the Year
Male Vocalist of the Year
Single of the Year ('A Boy Named Sue')
Vocal Group of the Year (with June Carter Cash)
2003 Album of the Year (*American IV: The Man Comes Around*)
Single of the Year ('Hurt')
Music Video of the Year ('Hurt')

Country Music Hall of Fame
1980: Inducted into the Country Music Hall of Fame

Gospel Music Hall of Fame
2011: Inducted into the Gospel Music Hall of Fame

Grammy Awards
1968: Best Country & Western Performance, Duet,
Trio or Group (with June Carter Cash, 'Jackson')
1969: Best Album Notes (*At Folsom Prison*)
Best Male Country Vocal ('Folsom Prison Blues')
1970: Best Male Country Vocal ('A Boy Named Sue')
1971: Best Country Performance by a Duo or Group
with Vocal (with June Carter Cash, 'If I Were
A Carpenter')

1995: Best Contemporary Folk Album (*American Recordings*)
1998: Best Country Album (*Unchained*)
1998: Grammy Hall of Fame Award ('I Walk The Line')
Grammy Hall of Fame Award ('Ring Of Fire')
1999: Grammy Lifetime Achievement Award
2001: Best Country Male Vocal ('Solitary Man')
2003: Best Country Male Vocal ('Give My Love To Rose')

Hollywood Walk of Fame
1960: Awarded star on the Hollywood Walk of Fame

MTV Video Music Awards
2003: Best Cinematography ('Hurt')

Nashville Songwriters Hall of Fame
1977: Inducted into Nashville Songwriters Hall of Fame

Rock and Roll Hall of Fame
1992: Inducted into Rock and Roll Hall of Fame

Songwriters Hall of Fame
1977: Inducted into Songwriters Hall of Fame

ONLINE

www.johnnycash.com
Official site for the Man In Black.

www.johnnycashonline.com
Official fansite of Johnny Cash, log in to see what other fans are talking about or keep up with the latest Cash news.

facebook.com/johnnycash
With over 12 million likes, log in to see what others are saying about Cash.

www.thejohnnycashproject.com
A global collective art project in honour of Johnny Cash.

BIOGRAPHIES

Helen Akitt (Author)
Helen Akitt is a teacher, writer and musician, with a special interest in US popular culture and roots music. She has annotated CD reissues by artists as celebrated and diverse as Bob Dylan, Woody Guthrie, Pete Seeger, Joan Baez and Willie Nelson. Her publications have profiled such screen icons as Clint Eastwood and Doris Day, while she has also written about the golden age of the Hollywood Western.

Paul Du Noyer (Foreword)
Paul Du Noyer began his career on the *New Musical Express*, went on to edit *Q* and to found *Mojo*. He also helped to launch *Heat* and several music websites. As well as editing several rock reference books, he is the author of *We All Shine On*, about the solo music of John Lennon, and *Wondrous Place*, a history of the Liverpool music scene. He is nowadays a contributing editor of *The Word*.

PICTURE CREDITS